Original title:
Stories in the Floorboards

Copyright © 2025 Creative Arts Management OÜ
All rights reserved.

Author: Maxwell Donovan
ISBN HARDBACK: 978-1-80587-019-7
ISBN PAPERBACK: 978-1-80587-489-8

Whispers of the Weight Above

A creak in the night, what's that sound?
The cat is perplexed, spinning round.
Is it ghosts or a squirrel, doing a dance?
Or just Aunt May, lost in her pants?

Under the weight of our old wooden home,
The laughter and giggles, they like to roam.
A story in shadows, the light barely spills,
While grandma's old shoes dance over the hills.

What Lies Beneath the Finish

Beneath the varnish, what secrets may lie?
A rogue shoe has vanished, oh my, oh my!
Was it taken by elves or a whimsical mouse?
Or stuck to the glue of this creaky old house?

When the floorboards sigh, do they tell us a tale?
Of socks that got lost on a grand spinning gale.
Was a sandwich forgotten, or just crumbs of time?
Or is it a rhyme that has lost its chime?

Fragments of the Past

Old toys are scattered, each one a delight,
A soldier, a doll, all lost to the night.
But listen close now, and you might just find,
They giggle and whisper, with mischief aligned.

The dust bunnies hide secrets from days long ago,
Adventures galore, if only they'd show.
Was that a big tattle from the wooden old floor?
Or just the old vacuum, searching for more?

Haunting in the Halls

In corridors narrow, echoes do roam,
A phantom or two make this place feel like home.
A slip on a rug and a tumble told straight,
The ghosts laugh aloud at our jumbled fate.

With mischief afoot, the shadows have fun,
Playing hide and seek until the day is done.
A friendly old bump in the middle of night,
With each wobbly step, there's a giggle of fright.

Secrets Caught in Grain

In the creaks, old jokes reside,
Whispered laughs, a playful tide.
A mouse plays tag with a wobbly chair,
While dust bunnies giggle without a care.

Footsteps quicken, a dance through the hall,
Wooden knees crack, as shadows fall.
Each knot a tale, each scratch a grin,
What hidden mischief has wandered in?

Tales Trapped in Timber

Once a shoe fell, a slapstick show,
Landed on toes—oh, how they'd glow!
A cat rolled by, intrigued by the sound,
Pouncing on laughter, "Hey, that's profound!"

A spill of juice, a colorful tale,
Sticky-beaked birds, bandits without fail.
In the knots and grains, secrets do play,
As floorboards chuckle, they dance all day.

Beneath the Plank's Embrace

A squirrel once stashed an acorn up high,
But it rolled and it tumbled, oh my, oh my!
The laughter erupted from every nook,
As the critters all gathered to have a look.

A prankster spider spun webs with flair,
While old Mr. Dustball twirled with a stare.
With rustling whispers, they plotted their schemes,
Floorboards alive with their whimsical dreams.

Murmurs of the Unseen

The old wood creaks a comedic tune,
When pets parade under the silver moon.
A wobbly table tells tales of its past,
Of children who danced and made childhood last.

In shadows they gather for chatter and jokes,
As floorboards chuckle at their little folks.
A ticklish breeze breezes through the cracks,
Mirthful secrets hidden, there's no looking back!

Grain and Echo

Beneath the floor, a secret world,
Where ghosts of dust bunnies swirl.
An echo of yesterday's goof,
Whispers of a misplaced roof.

Each creak a giggle, a playful sound,
As old friends dance all around.
Naps interrupted by funny snores,
As laughter tumbles through hidden doors.

The Fabric of the Floor

Tangles of thread in a warping seam,
Patchwork tales of a hidden dream.
Nuts and bolts, a mischievous band,
Sewing together a laughable land.

Old shoes with stories, they wiggle and sway,
With tales from yesterday, come out to play.
Beneath the rug where mischief thrives,
Funny critters live their lives.

The Hidden Residents

A family of mice in a tiny house,
Throwing parties that make us rouse.
Waltzing with crumbs on a bright cheese moon,
Their hoofed dance makes the floorboards croon.

They craft a hat from a thimble so grand,
A hidden festival, a playful band.
Under the beams, they giggle and cheer,
With tickles and squeaks, the joy is here.

Unearthed Whispers

Footsteps above are the songs of the past,
Where grumpy old planks creak and contrast.
Each crack a chuckle, each bump a sigh,
Echoes of life with a wink and a guy.

Lost socks are treasure, or so they say,
Whispered joys from a bygone day.
From the depths of timber, tales collide,
In fractured laughter, old secrets hide.

Cracks of Time

In the wood, a secret found,
Whispers of laughter all around.
Old shoes tapping, a silly dance,
Each creak a tale of happenstance.

A cat once slid with a pounce so grand,
Chasing shadows, as if planned.
With every step, the past comes alive,
As we giggle at how memories thrive.

The Dance of the Floor

Boots and slippers in a jive,
Spinning tales that come alive.
Watch the dust bunnies kick and sway,
In a goofy, pirouetting play.

A mischievous squeak as they hold tight,
Making mischief all through the night.
The lamp shakes, the pictures tilt,
In this floor, no lack of guilt.

Underfoot Reminiscence

Pitter-patter of little feet,
Chasing echoes, oh so sweet.
Who knew the floor could hold such fun,
With each step, a new pun begun?

A spill from lunch, a cookie's fate,
Mangled crumbs, an epic date.
Underneath, a treasure trove,
Of giggles and crumbs that we strove.

Resonance of the Forgotten

Echoes laugh from years gone past,
In the floor, they hold steadfast.
A silly wiggle, a shoe that squeaks,
Reminds us all how laughter peaks.

Dance with joy, let stories flow,
From boards beneath, their secrets glow.
With a tap and a twist, the past joins in,
In this wooden realm, we're bound to win.

Shadows of Unspoken Memories

In corners where the dust bunnies play,
A rogue shoe's tale gets lost in the fray.
A pair of old socks went out for a chat,
While missing one sandal just lounged on the mat.

The cat once held court, ruling the scene,
On a throne made of clutter, a soft feline dream.
Whispers of giggles blend with the creaks,
As old toys exchange their long-lost techniques.

Lurking Legends Underfoot

An army of crumbs staged a revolt,
While the rug's fibers spun tales with a jolt.
The keys to the memories jingle and jive,
As they dance with the dust, so happy and alive.

A ghost with a broom has plans of escape,
Collecting the secrets that no one can scrape.
In silence they linger, with laughter untried,
As the planks sashay in their wooden pride.

Fables of the Forgotten Floor

Beneath the old beams, a party was thrown,
With mice as the guests and the dust as their throne.
The old coffee cup sways to a tune,
While the spoons in the drawer sing out in June.

In shadows they giggle, a band of the lost,
Sharing their laughter without any cost.
The leftover pizza has tales of its own,
As it, too, recounts the laughter well-known.

Beneath the Surface: A Silent Chorus

Beneath the surface, a chorus of glee,
A tumble of stories no one can see.
The bubblegum pink that once left a stain,
Now welcomes the roaches to dance in the rain.

An old crayon sketches the joys of the past,
While splinters carry on, holding memories fast.
As squeaks and creaks form a vibrant ballet,
In the theater of chaos, they giggle away.

Murmurs from Below

When you tread lightly, hear the chuckle,
Old shoes gossip, making a buckle.
Squeaky tales of where they have been,
About a cat or maybe a queen.

Beneath the floor, a party ensues,
With spilled drinks and some old rubber shoes.
Jokes from the past, a waltz gone awry,
As lost socks tell tales of the pie in the sky.

Tap dance with floors, a laugh in the air,
Wood whispers secrets of wonders and dare.
The echoes of blunders, the slips and the spins,
Always leave room for the grins and grins.

So giggle along with this playful parade,
For each creak and each crack is a fun masquerade.
In laughter, they linger, in jokes, they will grow,
The whispers perplexed, from the depths down below.

Forgotten Footprints

In corners where dust collects, shy but bold,
Lies a comedy of footprints, tales untold.
The old man's slippers on a dance floor,
And tiny shoes from one cheeky chore.

Who stepped here last? Was it a dog?
Or maybe a frog, in a playful fog?
Socks without pairs join in for the fun,
With giggles and jigs, they buzz like the sun.

Each mark upon wood is a liquid laugh,
A scene from a play on the quirky path.
The scenes unfold, a cartoon parade,
While changelings and tilters dance in the shade.

So come join the waltz of whimsical kin,
Where each faded footprint tells us to grin.
For in every smudge and a scratchy embrace,
Is a tale of mischief in this lively space.

Chronicles Beneath the Surface

Below the surface, a jest begs to rise,
In ticklish whispers under the guise.
The old cat's nap turned into a stir,
While journals of dust sing a muted slur.

Under chair legs, the creaky archives,
Hold chronicles of laughs, where mischief thrives.
The old rocking chair keeps tally of yore,
From the spaghetti fight of days never bore.

With every scratch and every little pounce,
There's a narrative spinning, in a funny bounce.
The neighbors' cat and the neighbor's dog,
Charting a saga under the log.

So lean in and listen, embrace the delight,
For chronicles dwell in the tapestry's light.
With each peek beneath, there's more to explore,
A zany history that promises more!

The Dusty Archive of Timelessness

In the dusty archive of laughter and cheer,
Old mops and brooms hold stories sincere.
The clock on the wall gossips away,
While dusty curtains dance in their play.

Forgotten relics twinkle with pride,
As the old bench chuckles, a spot to hide.
A rebel toy soldier, with one eye askew,
Waits for flushes of joy to break through.

Silly sketches are etched in the grain,
Knock-knock jokes hidden, like candy canes.
A spoon serenades the forgotten pies,
While a mop sings ballads under the skies.

So look for the smiles where history's bred,
In every small crack where laughter has led.
For in this archive, timelessness thrives,
With tales of the quirky, where humor survives.

Sounds of the Unseen

When the cat leaps up at night,
The floorboards creak like old bones.
A chorus of laughter in fright,
Surely, it's ghosts—or just gnomes!

With every squeak, there's a tale,
Of hidden socks and lost shoe laces.
A treasure hunt in the detail,
Memory's dance in funny spaces.

The mice hold parties under lights,
Their cheese is aged and quite refined.
Each nibble echoes misplaced bites,
Leaving crumbs of laughs behind.

So listen closely, lend an ear,
To the giggles that float around.
In the wooden whispers, it's clear,
The past is lively—and spellbound!

Echoes in the Wood Grain

Once a pirate hid beneath,
From a parrot and his foe.
Now the tale lies soft and sheath,
In grooves where secrets flow.

A tap-dancing leaf from the tree,
Rattled by a startled breeze.
Could it be a spirit's spree,
Or just a squirrel's expertise?

The knocks and thumps make us grin,
As if the wood has taken flight.
Every sound's a plucky win,
With echoes roaming through the night.

Open your ears, do not fret,
For lively tales lay on the floor.
Find amusement, no need to sweat,
Each creak's a giggle to explore!

The Quiet History of Each Step

As I tiptoe through the hall,
The wood groans under my weight.
It seems to whisper and call,
'Careful now, don't tempt fate!'

Each shuffle, a history told,
Of kids who raced, and pets that pranced.
Yet every creak is smooth and bold,
Inviting laughs with every chance.

An eerie laugh of a chair,
Sounds like it's plotting a prank.
A shoe that slips, twirls in air,
Wishing for an unseen plank.

So step not quietly, my friend,
For the past teems with mischief here.
Let laughter linger, never end,
Each board holds joy, never fear!

Beneath the Dust and Dirt

Here lies a lost yo-yo from years,
Beneath the dust and old despair.
A small reminder, bringing cheers,
Of childhood's quirks, without a care.

The pesky broom always wants more,
Chasing tales of toys long gone.
Yet every sweep brings laughter's score,
As memories play with the dawn.

What do the shadows sense and see?
They giggle as the moments wake.
A faint reminder of glee,
In every dust pile, history's stake.

So let the dust dance where it may,
To tickle toes with whimsy sights.
For funny tales are here to stay,
In every corner, laughter ignites!

Shadows Lurking in Silence

Beneath the surface, secrets crawl,
In the quiet, they grin and sprawl.
Squeaks and creaks take on a dance,
As whispers play their daring chance.

A sock's escape, a shoe's retreat,
What stories could they share in heat?
A game of hide and seek unfolds,
With laughter lost, but never told.

A muddle of dust, a spider's spin,
In corners where weird tales begin.
Cheeky mice with wit so high,
They plot as humans pass on by.

Beneath the floor, the tickle and tease,
Of every step that aims to please.
They chuckle loud with every thud,
As we unknowingly make our flood.

The Timeless Echo

In creaking echoes, laughter rings,
Of tiny feet and joyful things.
A tap, a clap, what's that we hear?
Oh, just the past, it's drawing near.

A rubber duck, a lost ballet,
What other treasures would they say?
In playful winks and chancey spins,
The ghosts of joy forever grin.

So come along, do join the fun,
For every nook a tale run.
An encore here, a giggle there,
All bottled up beneath our care.

With every stomp, a rabble grows,
A merry crowd the woodwork knows.
And as we dance on former years,
The floorboard laughs are loud and clear.

Beneath Our Feet Lies Time

Footsteps echo, time's ballet,
With stories spun in a fun display.
A pirate's map or a knight's lost shoe,
Each secret holds a giggle too.

The dust bunnies play hide and seek,
While old shoes chuckle, "We're unique!"
With each new stomp, they start to cheer,
Join the parade—come lend your ear!

Scattered marbles and a toy train,
All whisper tales of sunshine and rain.
They twist and frolic, how they shine,
As we unknowingly steal their time.

Underneath, a carnival bright,
Where clowns and jesters come to light.
From wooden depths, the magic beams,
Enticing us within our dreams.

The Wooden Chronicles

Where old wood groans a silly tune,
And echoes flit like butterflies in June.
A cat's sly wink, a dog's soft bark,
They flirt with tales hidden in the dark.

Pine and oak share giddy laughs,
As old chairs plot their daring drafts.
In each groove, a giggle stays,
A raucous laugh from distant days.

They conspire with your every tread,
In secret meetings where cats are fed.
An army of dust bunnies engage,
In stories scripted upon their stage.

So dance and leap and rattle about,
For below, the fun runs without a doubt.
A carnival spun in knots of wood,
Where laughter thrived—oh, how it stood!

Unearthing the Past

Beneath the wood, a ticklish tale,
Where squeaks and creaks begin to wail.
A mouse named Fred, with boots so bright,
Danced through the night, what pure delight!

Old grandma's shoe, a slippered sight,
Once hid a secret—oh, what a fright!
A treasure trove of gum and dust,
Who knew the floorboards were so robust?

A cat named Whiskers, bold and brash,
Found candy wrappers in a flash.
He swiped them quick, with utmost glee,
As crumbs of laughter filled the spree!

So lift the planks and take a peek,
For in the cracks, the past will speak.
With chuckles shared, we'll dance once more,
In tales untold beneath the floor.

Grit and Grain

From splintered edges, chuckles burst,
As ants parade in comedic thrust.
They carry crumbs as big as their heads,
Creating chaos in their edible spreads.

A bowl of soup—spilled right away,
Rolling on floorboards to join the play.
With each tiny splash, a story's shared,
Of kitchen mischief, where no one cared!

Lost socks galore, a mismatched spree,
Danced with the dust, just wild and free.
They giggled together in shades of blue,
As the floor groaned softly and laughed too!

So let's embrace the quirky sounds,
Where laughter lies and silliness abounds.
These grains of joy beneath our feet,
Hold secrets of chuckles in every beat.

Footfalls Through History

Each step we take, a playful tap,
The floorboards respond with a giggle or clap.
A traveler's journey, in shoes aged and worn,
Makes music together, from dusk until morn.

A tap dance here, a skip over there,
Worn soles whisper tales of flair.
As boots stomp loudly, the echoes parade,
In the rhythm of life where memories cascade.

The squeak of mischief, a secret revealed,
An unknown delight long concealed.
With each footfall, the past dances too,
In a funny jive we all can pursue!

Bringing forth laughter from beneath,
Where every shuffle's a whimsical wreath.
We'll shimmy through time, no need to be shy,
With floorboards that giggle as we pass by.

The Stories We Stand Upon

Beneath our feet, a jolly band,
Of wiggly worms and dust so grand.
They wiggle and giggle with every shove,
Making history fun, like a hand-in-glove.

A dinosaur tiny made of old wood,
Through creaky doors, he's misunderstood.
With each little stomp, he wobbles about,
Waving his tail with a cheerful shout!

Sock puppets hiding in nighttime's embrace,
Practicing lines, playing their grace.
They put on a show right under the bed,
While laughter erupts from the words left unsaid.

So tap your shoes and sway to the call,
For there's mischief and magic in this hall.
We'll dance with the past, it's no big deal,
As stories beneath us begin to reveal.

Revealed Beneath the Boards

Beneath the wood where shadows creep,
A dancing cat, a secret leap.
An old lost shoe, a squeaky toy,
These hidden things bring lots of joy.

A sock that vanished, a rogue old hat,
They tell of mischief with a chat.
A tiny mouse on a quest tonight,
Looking for crumbs in the pale moonlight.

A ghostly giggle, faint but near,
Laughter echoes, full of cheer.
The floorboards creak, they can't be tamed,
Whispers fun, and none are blamed.

So here we dance on hardwood sheen,
With tales of shenanigans unseen.
Each step a beat, a joyful sound,
In this world where fun is found.

Tales That Time Forgot

Underneath where no one peeks,
Lie secrets wrapped in dusty streaks.
A sandwich stashed, not quite a treat,
And bubble gum worn thin on the seat.

Once a rogue cat, now long since gone,
Stole spoons at night, the little con.
Each creaky plank a giggle holds,
Of shoe sizes and brave young souls.

A lost toy dragon, a teddy bear,
Still they plot from their hidden lair.
Gathering mischief with little glee,
As they scheme beneath, oh can't you see?

There's humor thriving in every tale,
With laughter hidden on this old trail.
We step on stories, a joyful prance,
As floorboards echo our jolly dance.

Whispers Beneath the Surface

Once a young lad, a curious plight,
Stowed his treasures away for the night.
A marble here, a crayon there,
Lurking beneath with whimsical flair.

Old wallabies snooze where secrets dwell,
Pondering stories, they giggle and tell.
With crumbs for company and tales in tow,
The funny whispers in moonlit glow.

An alien sock from a distant land,
Tricked by the folks, with mischief planned.
Under the floor where dreams entwine,
An army of giggles, oh how they shine!

So when you tread on this aged ground,
Listen closely for laughter all around.
A chorus of joy from the depths below,
With delightful tales in their funny flow.

Echoes of Hidden Paths

Three pancakes stacked beneath the floor,
A feast forgotten, who could ask for more?
Beneath the cracks where giggles roam,
The funny little quirks of home.

Old Mr. Mouse, with a hat askew,
Pops by for crumbs and a dance or two.
Each step there holds a glimmering glee,
As tales of laughter float wild and free.

A rubber duck, once bright and bold,
Rides the currents of tales untold.
Adventures await where dust bunnies play,
As echoes of mirth pave the way.

So slide your feet on this wooden stage,
With each creak a tale of a witty age.
The whispers in shadows bring joy and art,
As this merry life sparks the heart.

Memories Etched in Pine

Beneath the old oak, laughter rings,
A dance of shadows, and that sings.
Silly secrets, lost and found,
In every creak, a tale unbound.

With every stomp, a ghost does cheer,
A tap for joy, a skip for fear.
The cat's surprise, a mouse that dodges,
While grandma's quilt, the floor it smudges.

A hidden gem in dusty lanes,
Timid treasures, a pint of games.
A jiggle, a wobble, the boards reply,
As dreams take flight, and giggles fly.

They shake like jelly, the house beams bright,
With whispers of children chasing night.
Each plank a purpose, each knot a grin,
In the heart of the home, laughter begins.

Echoes of the Forgotten

A shoe that squeaks, a door that yawns,
Echos of laughter greet the dawns.
Once lost to time, they wiggle free,
Whispers of nonsense, oh, let's agree!

Under the rug, a treasure tussled,
Where socks unite and lint is rustled.
Silly patches, stories born,
In quirks and quirks, all forlorn.

Fingers tap dance on dusty beams,
Like little fairies living in dreams.
Tales of mishaps, a hoot of surprise,
As boots and sandals play at disguise.

A rumble and tumble, the floors lament,
The secrets shared, the days well spent.
With every step, we dance anew,
In echoes of laughter, just me and you.

Beneath the Silent Structure

With every thud, a giggle heard,
Under our feet, a world deferred.
A puddle of memory, a shake, a span,
Where floorboards whisper of old-time plans.

Jumping and jiving, the echo's bright,
In forgotten corners, pure delight.
Dancing with shadows, we spin and glide,
While chipmunks gawk with eyes open wide.

Swaying and creaking, the secrets tell,
Of silly games played where they fell.
Each knot holds a secret, a laugh, a cheer,
Past misadventures always near.

Under our toes, they wiggle and play,
In mischief and giggles, they frolic and sway.
With a leap of joy on polished wood,
Beneath the silent, we find the good.

Rooted Remnants

Timber beams with stories to share,
Where laughter lingers, floating in air.
Silly sentiments in every groove,
A playful heart that yearns to move.

Wobbly chairs and squeaky floors,
In every corner, a memory roars.
Bubbles of laughter and whispers of glee,
In the roots of the wood, joy's decree.

Underneath the surface, life unfolds,
Tales of mischief, forever told.
Pudding dropped and tea that spilled,
In happy chaos, the space fulfilled.

Once sturdy planks now sprawl with grace,
A quirky dance in a tight-knit space.
With every crack and whimsy unfold,
The rooted remnants, a saga bold.

Unearthing Echoes of the Past

In the corners where shadows play,
Lies a tale of a cat's clumsy sway.
A thumping sound, then a squeal,
What secrets beneath those boards conceal?

Grandma lost her prize-winning pie,
Underneath, it did quietly lie.
The mice danced with crumbs on the floor,
While laughter echoed from door to door.

A jack-in-the-box peeks through a crack,
Startling memories, they bounce right back.
With squeaks and squeals, they start to tease,
Who knew wood held such wacky cheese?

Tap-tap goes the ghost of a shoe,
Stomping loudly with nothing to view.
The floorboards chuckle, their voices strange,
Encapsulating a world that won't change.

Footfalls in the Dust

Tiny feet scamper in the dark,
Chasing shadows where critters embark.
A thud, a bump, then a squeaky sigh,
What silliness makes the old floorboards cry?

The dog's antics leave old walls laughing,
While dust bunnies go a-dancing and crafting.
A bump and a thump from the attic above,
Maybe a monster that's searching for love?

Each thistle and creak brings giggles anew,
The floor's own symphony, just for you.
Mice in top hats play a grand show,
Feet tapping rhythm, waltzing to and fro.

Beneath every splash of that playful grime,
Lies a history told in mismatched rhyme.
Where do they come from, these sounds and feats?
The floorboards will giggle, as sun gently greets.

The Language of the Lattice

A lattice of whispers, a council of squeaks,
Discussing the chaos that mischief seeks.
Echoes of giggles arise from the seams,
Slipping through slats into bright summer dreams.

Beneath the old table, a ruckus ignites,
As critters concoct their grand little flights.
Bouncing with laughter, they play hide and seek,
Squealing together, their plans are not meek.

With each little shuffle, a story unfolds,
The charm of the past, with mischief it molds.
A treasure of whispers, a world to explore,
The wooden tales bloom forevermore.

Tick-tock goes the clock, yet time stands still,
As goodies await under old window sill.
Laughter and mischief in every crevice,
In the language of wood, it's pure cleverness.

Where the Old Meets the New

Old boots and new shoes dance side by side,
Creating a rhythm with every stride.
The floorboards chuckle with every beat,
What tales they could tell of the feet they greet!

The cats weave tales through the threads they pursue,
Sneaking and swaying, so sprightly and true.
While the old chair groans under the weight,
Of laughter and memories that never abate.

Grandpa's slippers, so fluffy and worn,
Tell of adventures from dusk until dawn.
While little ones tumble and topple with glee,
Rattling the roots of our ancestry.

So here's to the clash of the past and the bright,
To echoes that giggle and dance with delight.
As floorboards beneath us tell stories anew,
Where laughing together makes all old things new.

Rustling Resilience

In the hush of night, things giggle and creak,
Whispers of laughter, old wood's unique.
Each scratch and scuffle a tale to behold,
A dance of the past, in the floors made of gold.

Crackers for mice, and whispers of cheer,
Scurrying stories that only we hear.
A waltz of the dust, a jig with the light,
Toe-tapping tunes in the heart of the night.

Beneath every board, the mischief we find,
Tickles and tales that tickle the mind.
Quirky companions, the resident sprites,
In the dullness of day, they ignite with delights.

So next time you trip, just give it a grin,
For the floors are alive with the fun that's within.
Beneath our two feet, the oddities gleam,
Creating a life more peculiar than dream.

Threshold of Memories

At the edge of the room, oh what fun waits,
Tales of old laughter, of whimsy and fates.
The floorboards remember each groove and each pat,
They chuckle with glee, underfoot, like a cat.

A misstep in the hall causes laughter to roar,
As shoes slip and slide, like a comedic chore.
The past prances back in each squeak and each groan,
In a play of the ages, the floor's the throne.

Worn shoes whispered tales of each party, each dream,
From love at first sight to a spilled soda stream.
Every crack holds a giggle, a wink from the past,
In a dance of remembrance, the moments are cast.

So here we stand still, at this threshold of lore,
Collecting the laughter that settles and soars.
In the shadows, they linger, our echoes in tow,
A raucous parade that the floorboards bestow.

Where the Dust Settles

In the corners so cozy, where sunlight can't stare,
Lives a chorus of chuckles, a lighthearted air.
Dust bunnies convene for a waltz in the gloom,
As they spin 'round the table in a whimsical room.

Forget not the duster's forlorn little plight,
Fighting a battle with all of his might.
Each swipe told a story of missing a place,
A tumble, a giggle, a rather wild chase.

The tick-tock of memories feels playful and round,
Every shake and each shimmy, soft laughter abound.
In the breeze that slides by, with each festooned twirl,
Dust settles on smiles in this magical whirl.

So, take off your shoes, let your worries unwind,
And dance on the flakes that the sunlight has lined.
Life sparkles beneath where the dust chooses to lay,
In a footprint of joy that won't ever decay.

The Silent Archive

In the depths of the floor, where the quiet resides,
Sit tales of mischief, like secrets and guides.
With every new stomp, the old tales awake,
A library of giggles with every footstep we make.

Socks go on adventures, they wander and roam,
Finding lost Lego pieces, creating a home.
Sir Floors-a-Lot guards the treasure below,
In the dusty old cracks where the wild stories grow.

Pranks on the cat, as they tumble and fall,
The books of the past gather dust on the wall.
They chuckle at socks that have gone missing too,
In a whimsical dance where the heartfelt comes through.

So here in this space, let your laughter ignite,
In the hushed silent archive, where chaos feels right.
Each corner a chapter, a page that won't bend,
In the floors of our laughter, there's magic to send.

Whispers Beneath the Planks

Little critters dance and play,
Rumors fly the night away.
Underneath the creaky beams,
Laughter hides in silly dreams.

A mouse in boots, a cat with flair,
Twist and twirl without a care.
They tell their tales in tiny squeaks,
Nightly feasts last for weeks!

With every creak, a giggle breaks,
As mischief stirs from slumber's lakes.
The floor can't hold their vibrant cheer,
For laughter spills over here.

So tread with joy, don't make a fuss,
For you might catch a glimpse of us!
Floorboards grinning, creaking wide,
Join the fun, come take a ride.

Echoes of Hidden Paths

A tale of squeaky shoes doth roam,
While split wood dreams of a home.
Underneath where dust bunnies hide,
Chuckle-faces peek and slide.

Flip-flops squeal, and slippers hum,
As secret dances make you come.
Frogs in tuxedos leap and bound,
While unseen hitchhikers dance around.

Jumps and skips between the frames,
An opera of forgotten names.
Step lightly or the shadows tease,
With joking whispers in the breeze.

So take your time on creaky floors,
Who knows what laughter still explores?
With echoes bouncing, never shy,
Find your rhythm, give it a try.

Secrets of the Subsurface

Underneath where no one sees,
Gossipy mice play as they please.
Ticklish waves caress the stone,
As echoes giggle, never alone.

Hiding socks and bits of fluff,
Adventures echo, some quite tough.
A plushy bear that rolled away,
Joins in games until the day.

Tapping shoes on wooden base,
Spinning tales at a frantic pace.
Mice are rangers, daringly brave,
Creating fun, the floors they wave!

So bow to the wood, give a cheer,
Hear the stories draw you near.
Though hidden well, they are quite clear,
In every creak, a giggle's here.

Tales Woven in Wood

With every step, a chuckle sends,
Old planks and beams are our best friends.
Tangled vines and knots expose,
Secrets wild that no one knows.

Invisible gnomes in hats so tall,
Dance on boards that gleefully call.
They flip and flop, and oh, what grace,
In hidden realms, they find their place.

Chirping crickets, all in line,
Hold parties under beams so fine.
Their silly songs ring through the night,
While lanterns flicker, shining bright.

So listen close to tales abound,
In every creak, giggles resound.
The floor holds more than steps we take,
It's laughter mixed in every shake.

History Underfoot

When you walk, the creaks will sing,
A tale of socks and things that cling.
Lost toys and crumbs from long ago,
   Tickling toes in a dance of woe.

Flip-flops whisper, 'Oh, not again!'
As dust bunnies plot their little den.
The vacuum's roar, a dragon's call,
Mighty heroes 'gainst the crumb-filled hall.

What do the fibers see and hear?
Adventures stuck from yesteryear.
A stomp from dad, and the floor shakes wide,
   While mom just laughs, oh what a ride!

So sway and slide upon the ground,
With giggles hiding in each sound.
The floorboards know our tiny fights,
And they'll keep laughing through the nights.

Ghosts of the Grit

In corners where the shadows play,
The dust and dirt begin to sway.
Old spatulas and spoons of wood,
Once cut the food, now laugh for good.

Silly ghosts in sweeping brooms,
Have crazy love for all the glooms.
Waltzing through the cobweb dance,
Gliding still, they take a chance.

Footfalls echo with a mischieve's grin,
As they plot and scheme with a cheeky spin.
Chasing tails like puppies do,
Creating messes just for you.

So next you tread on that old wood,
Remember, it's alive, just like it could.
With every step, a chuckle's found,
Where laughter dances all around.

The Heartbeat of House

Beneath the weight of everyday,
A heartbeat thumps in odd ballet.
With every footstep, it's quite the show,
Toppling stools and saying 'whoa!'

Curtains flutter at a dear old dance,
While chairs have sprouted phantom prance.
The echoes of laughter softly blend,
With creaky floors that twist and bend.

Watch how the walls hum their tune,
As carpet fibres become a swoon.
Every thud and bump like a jolly beat,
Befriending mischief at our feet.

So listen in, let laughter soar,
The house has stories like never before.
In the rhythm of life, find joy and cheer,
In this raucous home, let's not disappear.

Threads Woven Through Wood

The floor sings tunes of a lively band,
With threads that twist and keep it grand.
They weave together tales of snacks,
From pop-tarts to crumbs in little packs.

A treadle of socks and mismatched shoes,
Where fun and chaos softly fuse.
Each creak delights with hints of glee,
Saying to me, 'Come dance with me!'

Mice make plans in a hasty flight,
Scurrying 'neath the glow of light.
Who knew the floor could throw a party?
Where laughter stirs and beats quite hearty?

So step lightly on this playful ground,
Let chortles of joy forever abound.
For woven tales in wood and grain,
Are the footprints of laughter that shall remain.

The Forgotten Treads

When I walk on this old wood,
It squeaks like it's in the mood.
Echoes of laughter fill the air,
As if ghosts are giggling everywhere.

Beneath my feet, they dance and sway,
Conjuring memories of yesterday.
From clumsy kids to mischief grand,
Each dent and scratch tells stories unplanned.

Oh, how the floor has seen it all,
From endless games to a drink's great sprawl.
With every thump, it grins and creaks,
It's got more secrets than we could ever peek.

So here I stand, a witness to time,
A traveler lost in the rhythm and rhyme.
With each step forward, I can't help but chuckle,
For life's a funny little wood-plank shuffle.

Stories in the Silences

In the quiet spaces where shadows cling,
The floor whispers tales that make me swing.
With creaks and moans, it starts to share,
All the funny things that linger in the air.

A crumb or two, a lost old sock,
Beneath the boards, they giggle and mock.
Little ninjas with giggly retreats,
Playing hide-and-seek in mysterious beats.

Dust bunnies gather and throw a ball,
While the floorboards chuckle, standing tall.
What once was serious, now seems absurd,
With every stumble, I'm sharing a word.

So here I dance, and here I sway,
With some laughter from the wood, come what may.
For every silence carries some fun,
And the floor makes sure we're never done.

Underneath, a World Awakens

Under the floor, the critters convene,
In a lively world that's rarely seen.
With tiny feet scurrying to and fro,
They plot their tricks in a playful show.

Old nails rattle, they tap a beat,
While the dust motes dance in their little suite.
Squeaks turn to laughter, a furry parade,
In this hidden land where mischief is made.

I hear the pitter-patter, their joyous sound,
Making memories where laughter is found.
With every shuffle, a giggle bursts,
And the floor sings loud, quenching our thirsts.

So next time you walk with a curious glance,
Remember the floor is hosting a dance.
With secrets so spry and moments so bright,
We join in their mirth, and everything's right.

Footprints of the Past

Each scuff and mark tells a tale from long,
Of slipping feet where they don't belong.
The cat made strides, oh, what a show,
Across the hall, a slippery go.

In the middle of the night, a snack attack,
Left crumbs that now on the board walk slack.
With careful steps, the midnight sneaks,
Return with joy, and the floor still squeaks.

It knows of giggles and secret snacks,
Of tiny thuds and unexpected cracks.
Memories echo with every tread,
While the floor boards smile, never misled.

So dance on paths that others made,
Leave your own mark; don't be afraid.
For every footstep is a laugh, it seems,
We're all part of the floor's funny memes.

Beneath the Layers of Dust

There's a rumor whispered low,
That the dust bunnies put on a show.
With tiny shoes and a grand parade,
They twirl and leap, completely unafraid.

Underneath the old floorboards,
They throw raucous parties with tiny chords.
Champagne bubbles made from crumbs,
While the furniture quietly hums.

Each speck of dust tells a tale,
Of a time when the cat went pale.
When the dog danced like a pro,
And the broom would join in the flow.

So if you hear a little thump,
It's just the dust bunnies having a jump.
With giggles hidden from plain sight,
They keep it lively every night.

Ancestral Footsteps

Once I found a boot from the past,
With tales of grandpa's life so vast.
It tapped and winked, a jolly prank,
Claiming he danced as if a flank!

A feather fell from a hat so tall,
Said it witnessed a tumble and a fall.
In each creak, there's a chuckling voice,
From ancestors who made quite the noise.

The echoes of laughter fill the air,
As they plot their next big flair.
They conspire to wiggle and jive,
In the corners where old ghosts thrive.

So dance with me, oh spirits old,
We'll celebrate mysteries yet untold.
In the nooks, their joy survives,
In each beat, the laughter thrives.

The Hidden Narrative

A squeaky floorboard told a joke,
Of a spider who learned to poke.
He claimed he spun tales of romance,
While everyone else tried their dance.

Underneath the table's swell,
A gopher shared a grand tale well.
About a nut that slipped away,
And danced all night till break of day.

Behind the planks, the laughter swells,
With every creak, a story tells.
There's a whisper, a chuckle, a sigh,
As tales take flight and then they fly.

So join the floorboard's merry show,
Where imagination steals the glow.
With every step, they light the way,
For mischief and laughter come what may.

Lost Voices in the Woodwork

In the woodwork, voices tease,
Chattering tales carried by the breeze.
A moth recites a dramatic play,
While the hammer nods in dismay.

A splinter says, 'I was a tree!'
Echoing laughter, so free and glee.
Whispers of wormy antics delight,
With stories that sneak into the night.

The glue pot's grumble is a roar,
Of mishaps and blunders from before.
Every crack sings of fun past,
With each little thump, the shadows cast.

So lend an ear to the wooden choir,
Where lost voices never tire.
In their laughter, joy won't cease,
In each little squeak, there's pure fleece.

Chronicles of the Undercurrent

Beneath the floor, there's quite a show,
Dust bunnies waltz, putting on a glow.
Crumbs from dinner, a feast so grand,
Ants are the guests with a marching band.

Squeaky boards laugh at every step,
Telling tales of the secrets kept.
Invisible friends at play all night,
Their giggles drift in the dim moonlight.

Mice hold meetings in hidden corners,
Debating over who's the funniest warner.
The cat on duty, a fumbled spy,
Turns clueless as whispers pass by.

In these depths of mischief and cheer,
Lies a world where joy draws near.
With every creak, there's much to see,
A giddy realm of harmony.

The Life Beneath

Where cobwebs dance and shadows play,
Lies a bustling town, come what may.
Spiders spin tales that tickle and tease,
While roaches pirouette with expert ease.

A raucous band of beetles rejoice,
Strumming their guitars, they make some noise.
Every thump of a shoe overhead,
Is a soap opera, eagerly fed.

The mouse brigade parades with flair,
Chasing each other without a care.
They crash through crumbs like a food festival,
Each nibble savored, feeling so special.

In this underground circus, so bright,
Life's a laugh, a comical sight.
Amidst the chaos, cheerfully found,
The laughter below is the joy all around.

Oak-Hearted Whispers

Old floorboards creak with a knowing grin,
Sharing secrets, where laughter begins.
There's a family of squirrels, bold as can be,
Holding a weekend film fest, oh what glee!

Acorns are popcorn, to munch and delight,
As they watch shadows dance in the dim light.
The wood chuckles softly, feeling so wise,
Recalling those pranks and sweet surprise.

A family of mice performs every night,
Dressed in leaf costumes, they put on a fight.
Their heroic tales, amid giggles and cards,
To the wooden stage, cheers and claps of hearts.

With oak as a backdrop, dreams take flight,
Under the floor, oh what a sight!
Here in this chamber of giggles and glee,
Life spins its yarns, oh joyfully free.

Secrets in the Slats

Underneath where the children play,
Crickets chirp in a glamorous ballet.
A raccoon joins, wearing a hat,
Telling each secret he overheard spat.

Squeezed between wooden slats and gaps,
Lies a world buzzing with jokes and laughs.
The dust motes swirl as if in a dance,
While each creature spins tales of chance.

A lost sock leads a rebellion, you see,
With lint as their spy, they laugh with glee.
A concert of squeaks for the shadows to hear,
Building a ruckus without any fear.

In the laughter beneath, joy knows no bounds,
As mischief and fun become the real sounds.
So remember, when you feel a thud,
It's simply the laughter, concealed in the mud.

Whispers of Yesterday

Beneath our feet, the boards do creak,
Tales of laughter, secrets they seek.
A squirrel's dance, a cat's grand leap,
Echoes of mischief, in shadows deep.

A lost sock whispers, 'Where have you been?'
Worn out shoes hiding where they've been.
Dust bunnies giggle, a fluffy parade,
In a world where memories never fade.

The furniture sighs, it knows the score,
A broomstick chase and an open door.
Every scratch tells of a trip or a fall,
With each little squeak, it's a party for all!

So next time you walk, give a nod to the floor,
It's a stage for the jesters, a trapdoor for lore.
Just listen closely, you might hear a tune,
From the lively past that keeps dancing till noon.

Unearthed Threads of Time

What lurks beneath, where dust bunnies roam?
An old cat's collar and a kid's lost comb.
Each footstep brings giggles from days long ago,
As history's fibers begin to show.

Laughter gets trapped in corners so tight,
A humble old crumb sparkles with light.
Frayed edges of carpet whisper their tales,
Of slip-ups and tumbles, and triumphs that sail.

Spiders conspire to knit a good yarn,
A tangled web growing with each wild charm.
Beneath our soles, adventures run free,
A stage for the wackiest jubilee!

So walk with a twinkle, and dance with delight,
The ground is alive, full of joy and delight.
Old treasures await in shadows and dust,
With history's humor, we wander, we trust.

The Hidden Lives of Old Homes

Within aged planks, the giggles entwine,
Of little ones plotting and making a line.
The creaky old staircase, a race to the top,
With each little tumble, the laughter won't stop.

The plumbing pipes talk, they seem to recall,
When water was running and chaos did sprawl.
A rubber duck's float on a tide of old dreams,
Swimming through memories and whimsical schemes.

The walls seem to shimmer with stories untold,
Of socks gone missing, of secrets so bold.
Each scratch on the paint holds a moment of glee,
A playtime adventure just waiting to be.

So tiptoe around, but don't forget to prance,
For the floorboards invite you to join the dance.
Beneath every step, there's a giggle anew,
In homes filled with laughter, waiting for you!

Memory's Labyrinth Underfoot

In the maze of the house, the wood has a say,
A riddle of giggles that clutter the way.
Squeaky hinges mumble of cookies and crumbs,
While light-hearted whispers evoke giddy hums.

The floors are alive with colorful dreams,
With echoes of laughter bursting at seams.
Jumping from cushions, with silly delight,
A parade of past antics, oh what a sight!

Elders recall every dip and each dive,
Of bouncy little kids who just couldn't thrive.
The charm of the chaos, the joy of the mess,
In a tapestry woven with silliness.

So step with a grin, feel the tickle below,
Where the heartbeat of memories bursts to and fro.
Each creak is a chuckle, each crackle's a cheer,
In the labyrinth of laughter, hold dear those who're near.

The Woodland Diary

In a cozy nook where squirrels play,
A chipmunk writes of his wild day.
He spills his acorns, oh what a laugh,
While rabbits dance on a secret path.

Mice gather 'round for a late-night feast,
With dancing bugs, they claim the least!
A fox in a waistcoat serves the cheese,
While trees chuckle in the evening breeze.

The owl scribbles tales of the night,
While dreams take flight in the soft moonlight.
Every whisper of the leaves is heard,
A woodland diary, the merriest word!

With twigs and twine, they craft their lore,
From root to branch, there's always more.
In this joyous realm, laughter's the key,
A page-turning tale for you and me.

Every Step a Memory

Each creaky floorboard sings a tune,
Of little feet that bounced by noon.
A skipping child with shoes unlaced,
Leaves laughter in this happy space.

The cat, with mischief in its eyes,
Pounces on shadows, oh what a surprise!
It tiptoes lightly, thinking it's sly,
While the dog's antics make everyone cry!

Each step taken on this airy stage,
Is inked with giggles that never age.
From jumping jacks to moonlit hops,
Every echo winks and never stops.

With dance parties in the living room,
And dreaming big 'neath the stars' bright bloom.
Memories tread where spirits soar,
Leaving footprints forevermore.

The Unseen Canvas

Beneath my feet, a canvas lies,
With scribbles from days, oh how they fly!
A toddler's crayon, a pizza slice,
Artful chaos, isn't it nice?

Each scuff and scratch tells a cheeky tale,
Of pizza parties and a wide-eyed whale.
Dances with dust, the golden glow,
Painted with laughter, don't you know?

Cats pounce and fish swim on land,
While monsters wrestle, all perfectly planned.
This floor is a stage for imagination's play,
Where memories mingle and never stray.

With splatters of juice and cookie crumbs,
They turn to laughter; oh how it hums!
An unseen canvas, colorful and spry,
Where the heart dances and dreams go high.

Dusty Memoirs

In corners where shadows like to creep,
Lie dusty memoirs of times lost in sleep.
A rubber band ball that bounced so high,
A giggle from grandma that still flits by.

Here's a dinosaur, an ancient toy,
Known to every girl and boy.
From forts of pillows to blanket skies,
Each grain of dust holds forgotten highs.

With a sneeze and a cough, tales unfold,
Of superheroes and pirates bold.
In a whiff of dust, they whisper delight,
"Remember when we danced through the night?"

Amidst the clutter of playful trails,
Are hearty laughs and wild, hearty tales.
So tiptoe softly, hear the cheer,
For every dust bunny holds a memory dear.

Beneath the Surface

Underneath the slats we see,
Tiny tales of jubilee.
A gum wrapper stuck so tight,
Whispers shared in the dead of night.

A critter's laugh, a shoe's mishap,
Sock puppets form a funny trap.
In this wood, a twinkle's maze,
Life's dance hidden in a haze.

Mice gossip in a squeaky voice,
Every creak's a new choice.
Beneath the chaos, joys abound,
In hardwood lairs, fun is found.

So tread lightly, skip with glee,
The floorboards hold sweet jubilee.
With each step, more giggles flow,
The memories dance just below.

The Murmurs Underfoot

Listen close to the sneaky sounds,
Punny jokes as mischief bounds.
A pancake flip, a squeaky shoe,
Laughter bubbling, oh what a view!

A kitty tale of feline delight,
Chasing dust bunnies all night.
The floor crackles with silly cheer,
As bedtime stories quietly appear.

Wobbling chairs join in the fun,
A unicycle ride, oh what a run!
Murmurs rise from beneath the grain,
Bubbles of joy, laughter's gain.

Tippy toes on a midnight spree,
Every scuff, a new decree.
Underfoot, a playful gang,
In this realm, silliness sang.

The Floor's Quiet Recollections

Quiet echoes from the wood,
Telling secrets, misunderstood.
Each scuff tells a playful tale,
Of misadventures, laughter's sail.

A toy train's trip, a doll's ballet,
Giggles wrapped in a secret play.
Under rugs, a charade unfolds,
In creaky archives, funny golds.

Old shoes sing of grandpa's dance,
A wobble here, a silly prance.
The floor hums with jokes untold,
As shadows stretch and glee takes hold.

In every crack, a memory held,
Of snickers scattered, trust upheld.
These quiet thoughts remain alive,
In wood and laughter, we all thrive.

Tides of Time

Waves of laughter crash and sway,
Beneath our feet, they laugh and play.
Memory's tide ebbs, it flows,
Silly moments nobody knows.

Crumbs of joy beneath the chair,
Little secrets that float in air.
Each little plunge, a step in rhyme,
Carrying giggles through the brine.

Time may pass, but jokes don't fade,
In every nook, a prank is laid.
With each shuffle, a giggle flees,
As wood remembers with playful ease.

So dance upon this creaky sea,
And let the winks flow wild and free.
The tides of joy keep rolling in,
With every giggle, we begin again.

The Life Beneath Our Steps

A mouse named Clyde wears shoes too tight,
He dances nightly, what a silly sight!
He trips on crumbs and rolls on the floor,
His little jig brings laughter, that's for sure.

The ants throw parties, with crumbs as their feast,
They boogie and twirl, never break their lease.
With crumbs aplenty, they never feel dread,
A wild soirée beneath where we tread.

The dust bunnies plot in their fluffy, soft den,
They hold secret meetings, again and again.
With giggles and glee, they scheme and they plan,
A revolution of fluff, led by a brave fan!

The floorboards creak, with a comical song,
A squeaky chorus, they sing all day long.
In the life beneath, where laughter's the key,
It's a raucous ballet, wild and carefree.

Beneath the Weight of History

Old Mr. Plank collects tales on his way,
Of socks that went missing, lost toys that won't play.
He chuckles at whispers from toes that once strolled,
A history rich with secrets retold.

The lost marbles roll like a rogue ball of fate,
Dodge the cat's paws, think they're too late.
Like ancient explorers under the floor,
Each dent and each scratch holds a tale to adore.

A cricket takes notes as he hops down the hall,
Jotting down all the mischief, big and small.
He snickers at humans, with their strange little trips,
When they spill their snacks, he takes joy in their slips.

Underneath all the chaos, it's joy we find,
From teetering toddlers to tales left behind.
The weight of the ages, it's not all so dire,
It's laughter and fun that the past does inspire.

Ghostly Hues of Domestic Life

In the shadows of night, with giggles so spry,
The chairs tell tales as they wobble and sigh.
The ghost of a grandpa with an ironic twist,
Plays tricks on the cat, he can't be dismissed.

The toaster, it sparkles with crumbs of delight,
Challenging the kettle to dance through the night.
With a pop and a whistle, they share in the fun,
Creating a ruckus till morning's begun.

A phantom who loves to hide under beds,
Teasing the dog with playful, witty threads.
It giggles with glee as the pets all take flight,
A hilarious chase in the pale, softer light.

These hues of our lives, in shadows they gleam,
With laughter and mischief, like a whimsical dream.
In the corridors soft, where echoes are rife,
It's the comedy hour of domestic life.

The Lumber's Lament

A plank sighed softly, with a creak and a groan,
"I once was a tree, now I'm just wood alone."
But in his lament, there's laughter to find,
For he's the best bench where pals intertwined.

The beams chuckle madly at dust's little dance,
While splinters reminisce of their wild, youthful prance.
They've housed mighty books and shoes left behind,
Creating a tapestry of life entwined.

"Remember the times a kid stood on me?
I was his great ship; oh, how wild and free!"
The wood smirks with pride, though he's slightly worn,
Through cracks and through knots, his spirit is reborn.

So here's to the timber, so funny and true,
With moments he carries like the morning dew.
In the lumber's lament, we discover anew,
That laughter and joy live in all that we do.

www.ingramcontent.com/pod-product-compliance
Lightning Source LLC
Chambersburg PA
CBHW051735290426
43661CB00123B/458